Original title:
The Fruit Basket of Memories

Copyright © 2025 Creative Arts Management OÜ
All rights reserved.

Author: Victor Mercer
ISBN HARDBACK: 978-1-80586-411-0
ISBN PAPERBACK: 978-1-80586-883-5

Harvesting Moments

In the orchard of laughter, I tend to my trees,
Where bananas wear sunglasses, swaying in the breeze.
A pear cracking jokes, with a zesty wit,
And apples take selfies, a fruity little hit.

Each season brings giggles, like berries placed high,
A cantaloupe clown, just passing on by.
We juggle the memories, like citrus, you see,
And squeeze all the fun till it's juicy and free.

Pomegranate Dreams

Pomegranates whisper tales, of days long ago,
With seeds that burst out laughing, a spirited show.
A melon in a tutu, oh what a sight,
As grapes join the conga, dancing through the night.

Dreams of a fruit fight, so juicy and grand,
Tomatoes in helmets, all set to withstand.
With laughter resounding, we dive in so bold,
In this wacky adventure, memories unfold.

Berry-Stained Hues

Berries painted smiles, in colors so bright,
Raspberries do cartwheels, in morning light.
Blueberries giggle, as they trample the ground,
While strawberries sing, they're the best pals around.

The juice from our antics, it splatters and flies,
Like confetti of laughter, beneath sunny skies.
We feast on the moments, with sweetness galore,
As berry-stained hues bring us back for more.

The Essence of Time's Orchard

In the orchard of time, we pluck at the fun,
Where lemons serve lemonade, under the sun.
A kiwi in glasses, with wisdom to share,
And cherries just giggling, without a single care.

Memories like apples, all crisp and so bright,
As peaches tell stories, of whimsical flights.
We blend all our laughter, like smoothies divine,
In this fragrant retreat, our hearts intertwine.

Nectar of Yesteryear

The grapes of laughter swell,
In silly tales we tell.
Bananas slip and slide,
With joy we cannot hide.

Pie fights in the sun,
Cream and laughter run.
Remember when we danced?
In fruit, we chanced romance.

Peaches blushed so bright,
Under the moonlight.
Cherries on a spree,
Sipped from a tree.

Gorging on sweet glee,
Life's the grandest spree!
With each memory, cheer,
We toast the yesteryear.

Orchard of Echoes

In the orchard where we played,
All the fruit was homemade.
We heard the apples sing,
As we dodged the bees' sting.

Pigs in blankets, what a treat,
With laughter, laughter sweet.
Every tree had a tale,
Of a banana boat sail!

Caught in a fruit prank war,
Pie in the face galore!
Juicy giggles unfurled,
In this quirky, bright world.

Memories ripe and true,
Not a single one is blue.
Echoing through the years,
Our laughter drowns our fears.

Citrus Sunrise

The dawn brings zest to play,
In our own silly way.
Lemons dancing with glee,
As we sip on sweet tea.

Tangerines in a row,
With a cheeky glow.
Oranges peel away woes,
As laughter overflows.

Sunshine shining bright,
Every fruit feels right.
In this morning spree,
Joy is our jubilee!

With each citrus bite,
We feel pure delight.
Rising with the sun,
Let the fun times run!

Juices of Long-Lost Days

Sipping on memories sweet,
Time's a funky treat.
Pineapple hats we wore,
Running from the dinosaur.

Berries stained our clothes,
With laughter in our prose.
We carved smiles in the rind,
Reliving every kind.

Strawberries painted skies,
With mischief in our eyes.
Watermelon giggles loud,
We were so fruitfully proud.

In a blend of delight,
Our spirits took flight.
With juices overflowing,
The fun keeps on growing.

Chutney of Cherished Times

In the kitchen, jars align,
Filled with laughs and silly signs.
A pinch of stories, a dash of glee,
Like grandma's dance — oh, what a spree!

Spicy moments, sweet delight,
My brother's prank, what a fright!
Each scoop digs up joy we shared,
In chutney past, we were all impaired.

Picking the Past

At the market, I roam the stalls,
Choosing memories like ripe, round balls.
Each fruit a tale, each peel a grin,
Like the karaoke night — where to begin?

Strawberries burst with summer laughs,
While old bananas share our gaffes.
Picking them fresh, I can't refrain,
From tasting joy, and some mild pain.

Mementos in a Bowl

A bowl of memories, what a sight,
Pineapple slices, so shiny and bright.
With oranges giggling, peaches in tow,
It's a fruit party where silliness flows.

Grapes rolling off with a splashy sound,
While cherries throw shade, "We're too round!"
In this bowl, nostalgia's not dull,
Each bite reminds us — we're all a little full.

Unwrapping Old Flavors

Peeling labels, what do I find?
Flavors of laughter, so unconfined.
Tinned tidbits from long ago,
A recipe book with a side of woe.

Lemon zest and puns collide,
In jars of memories, joy can't hide.
Each flavor tells stories, oh so grand,
Life's a buffet — just grab a hand.

Rhubarb Reverie

In the garden where rhubarb did grow,
I stumbled upon a hat covered in dough.
The birds giggled sweetly, a sight so absurd,
While ants held a meeting, their plans were unheard.

A pie went missing, the culprit was clear,
A raccoon in a tux, sipping root beer.
He danced on the table, a real sight to see,
As we all laughed together, just rhubarb and me.

Orchard of Forgotten Laughter

In the orchard, where fruits wear a grin,
An apple played poker, and he always would win.
The pears were all chuckling, their jokes on repeat,
While cherries took selfies, a fruity retreat.

The berries would gossip, each rumor a blast,
About how the orange was once a real cast.
We'd roll in the grass, all giddy with cheer,
In this funny orchard, where nothing's austere.

Spilled Juice of Reminiscence

I spilled my juice, oh what a delight,
It formed a river, red, shiny, and bright.
Fish made of cherries began to parade,
While a cantaloupe drummer kept time with a spade.

A grapefruit slipped, taking all by surprise,
With lemony laughter and wide-open eyes.
We danced through the puddles, such joyous display,
In a world made of sugar, we giggled away.

Fruitful Dreams

In dreams full of fruit, I slipped on a peel,
A banana wearing shades said, 'What a great deal!'
The grapes were bartering for a swing in the air,
While melons debated if they'd fit in a chair.

Through orchards of whimsy, we all took a ride,
Kiwis on roller skates, our laughter our guide.
With every sweet moment, our joy did expand,
In a land where each fruit had a musical band.

Sappy Tales of Youth

In the garden of dreams we'd play,
Climbing trees till the end of the day.
Falling down, we'd laugh and roll,
Chasing shadows, that was our goal.

Sticky fingers from candy treats,
Racing bikes down the summer streets.
Silly songs filled the air with cheer,
Summer days seemed to last all year.

Fruits of laughter in sun-kissed light,
Every mishap felt oh-so-right.
With friends who'd never say goodbye,
Those juicy days still make me sigh.

Now we share these tales with glee,
Moments sprouted like a tall tree.
Each giggle etched in my heart's bloom,
Sweet echoes of youth still fill the room.

Juiced Thoughts

Sipping lemonade on a sunny porch,
Dreaming big while we tried to scorch.
Mom's fresh pies are an endless source,
Of laughter, love, and a sweet discourse.

We'd squirt each other with garden hoses,
Play hide and seek among the roses.
Fruit fights ended with sticky hands,
In our world, we made our own plans.

Peachy prayers and apricot hopes,
Life's wild ride had us on tightropes.
We'd gather 'round for a berry feast,
With sticky cheeks, we'd never cease.

Juiced-up tales that we share today,
With each memory, we laugh and play.
The sweetness of youth, our daily dose,
In laughter's embrace, we can't help but boast.

Flavors of Home

The kitchen buzzed with scents galore,
Baking pies that made us adore.
Grandma's cookies, a buttery treat,
Each bite tasted like pure golden heat.

Cherries splattered on kitchen walls,
Laughter ringing through the hall calls.
Whipping cream with splashes around,
Creating chaos, the best kind found.

Peeling oranges as we shared our dreams,
Silly stories bursting at the seams.
Fruit salad mixes with love so bright,
Family gatherings turned into light.

The flavor of home is wild and free,
Full of spinning tales and glee.
With every bite, a grin would bloom,
In our hearts, there's always room.

Petal-Scented Memories

Under cherry blossoms, we would run,
Counting petals, oh, so much fun.
Giggles echoed through springtime air,
With twirls and jumps, we wiped our care.

Butterfly kisses and dandelion wishes,
Finding magic in childhood's riches.
Drinking nectar as the sun would rise,
We'd create laughter, no need for disguise.

In the garden where we'd often play,
Flower crowns made our worries stray.
Oh, the mischief that came with the blooms,
Still brings smiles and bedtime tunes.

Remember those days, oh how they gleam,
Petal-scented friendships fuel our dream.
With blossoms and laughs, our spirits soar,
In every heart, there's always more.

Bittersweet Harvest

In the orchard, apples fell,
One squashed my toe, oh what the hell!
Cherries giggled, the peaches cheered,
But my fruit salad idea quickly disappeared.

Bananas slipped, did a little dance,
Caught on video, my second chance!
Pineapple grins under sunny skies,
Who knew this bounty could lead to sighs?

Grapes rolled like marbles, a silly mess,
Squished in laughter—who could've guessed?
Every fruit holds a tale so sweet,
Yet here we are, strapped to our seats.

With every bite, a chuckle stays,
Mangoes whisper wild, funny ways.
In this patch of joy, we all relate,
Harvesting giggles, our funny fate.

Confessions of the Orchard

In whispers low, the trees confessed,
That while they grew, they never guessed.
They'd hear such tales of human blunders,
Falling over, all kinds of wonders.

The pears looked down with wobbly pride,
When I tripped on roots and nearly died.
Berries snickered, in crimson hues,
While I wiped off dirt from my shoes.

Lemons frowned, feeling quite sour,
As I juggled fruits for a whole hour.
With every slip and flail, I spied,
A secret world of fruit-filled pride.

And now it seems, this orchard laughs,
At silly moments and weird mishaps.
Together we share a comical spin,
In the sunshine's glow, our tales begin.

The Last Bite of Laughter

At the picnic table, joy was ripe,
We raised our mugs, took a little dip.
But then a fruit fly, quite the prank,
Whispered sweet nothings, right in my tank!

Watermelon's sweetness hid a seed,
Which made me jump, oh how it freed!
Tomatoes blushing, spilling their juice,
Our laughter erupted, what a raucous truce!

In the chaos, a pie took flight,
Gathering dreams in a frosty bite.
Oh, the crust was crisp, oh, so divine,
But my fork was missing! Oh, what a sign!

The crumbs of laughter danced around,
As we're swept away in joy profound.
One last bite left, the laughter stays,
As fruit-filled antics brighten our days.

Orchard's Embrace

Nestled between trees, we found a space,
Laughing among fruits in a wild embrace.
Plums were giggling, ripe with glee,
As we told tales of silly me.

Each berry told secrets, juicy and bold,
Of past adventures that never got old.
Peaches whispered stories, soft and sweet,
Of clumsy falls and forgotten feet.

With every crunch, we reminisced,
Of silly moments; oh, how we missed!
Bananas shared laughs from the tops of limbs,
While oranges chimed in with fruit-filled whims.

Our orchard grew loud with mirth and sunshine,
In this quirky haven, we take our time.
Together we bloom in laughter's grace,
In the orchard's heart, we find our place.

Seeds of Remembered Days

In a garden of giggles, we planted our dreams,
With terrible jokes, or so it seems.
Each seed that we sowed, a laughter's reply,
Growing tall with each pun, reaching up to the sky.

We watered the plants with sugary spright,
Danced in the sunlight, oh what a sight!
But weeds of embarrassment sprouted in rows,
As we laughed 'til we cried, who knew how it goes?

The fruit of our folly, so ripe and so sweet,
Brought memories flooding, like a runaway fleet.
Oh, to recall, how we tumbled and rolled,
In our patch of hilarity, bold stories unfold.

So here's to the laughs and the moments we shared,
In the garden of memories, we always declared.
Each seed, planted happily, still gives us delight,
In the harvest of smiles that shine ever bright.

The Orchard of Lost Laughter

In an orchard where giggles fell from the trees,
We gathered the chuckles, breezy as a tease.
The apples were jokes, the pears were a pun,
Each bite took us back to when laughter was fun.

But some fruits were sour, with cringes unseen,
Recalled in our minds like a bad movie scene.
The laughter it brought, a sweet-lemon surprise,
As we held our bellies and squeezed our eyes.

With branches of memories weighed down by the past,
We tossed out the lemons, oh boy, what a blast!
Each tumble on vines, with skinned knees and glee,
Became part of the harvest that shaped you and me.

So let's stroll through this orchard, make memories anew,
In the shade of our chuckles, we'll find sparkling dew.
Together we'll wander, hand in hand it feels right,
In the orchard of laughter, our hearts take flight.

Tasting Time's Delights

A bowl filled with stories, ripe for a bite,
Each fruit, a reminder of a glorious night.
The cherries of chaos, the peaches of glee,
Each taste brings a chuckle, a moment we see.

Bananas of blunders, so slippery and slick,
They peel back the years, oh what a neat trick!
With every crunch taken, the flavors unfold,
A banquet of laughter, more precious than gold.

The grapes of good times ferment, aged and sweet,
Nostalgia in sips, it's a bubbly treat.
We toast to the mishaps, the tempests and storms,
In this feast of remembrance, our laughter transforms.

So come join our tasting, bring joy to the mix,
With every small nibble, we share all the tricks.
In this flavor-filled journey, we'll savor delight,
Following laughter's trail, shining luminous and bright.

Slices of Yesterday

In a pie made of laughter, all sliced up just right,
Each wedge tells a story, bringing back light.
The crust made of giggles, the filling of joy,
Reminds me of when we were just girls and a boy.

The cherries on top, a sprinkle of fun,
Each bite full of memories, oh, how we've run!
Through fields of amusement, so wild and free,
Chasing down shadows, just you and me.

So let's grab a fork and savor the past,
With slices of laughter, our memories cast.
These flavors of friendship will never go stale,
In our cookbook of life, we'll always prevail.

With each tasty piece, we'll laugh and we'll cheer,
For every loud moment that brings us near.
In a slice of forever, we'll cherish the blend,
Of hilarious stories that never will end.

The Poetry of Orchard Paths

On a path where apples bop,
I stole a peach and took a hop.
The trees they whispered, 'What a clown!'
A giggle here, let's gather round.

I plucked a pear, it slipped, oh dear!
My laughter rang, it filled the sphere.
Bananas danced like they were mad,
As memories grew, both good and bad.

Fragrant Chronicles of Life

In a garden bursting bright,
I tripped over a fruit's delight.
The berries laughed as I slipped through,
Splat! What a sight, my face was blue!

Peaches rolled and oranges spun,
This chronicle was way too fun.
With every slip, a story bloomed,
Even the dust, in joy it loomed.

A Tapestry of Flavorful Moments

In the tapestry of juicy bites,
I tangled up in fruit-filled nights.
Grapes tried to wrap me in their vines,
While cherries teased with bold designs.

With laughter stitched in every thread,
I danced with figs until I fled.
To spice and sweet, my heart would soar,
These moments lived, I always crave more.

Gathering Memories from the Tree of Time

With a basket perched on my head,
I scrambled back, but tripped instead.
A mango bonked me on my knee,
No wonder fruits are wild and free!

As memories fall like autumn leaves,
I chuckle at the bag of thieves.
Oranges giggle, apples sway,
In the orchard where we laugh and play.

Plums of the Heart's Longing

Once I found a plum so bright,
Ate it whole, oh what a sight!
But my face turned quite the shade,
I've been told I'm quite the trade.

It squished and dribbled down my chin,
My friends all laughed, 'That's quite the win!'
Yet in that silly, fruity mess,
A sweet reminder of happiness.

Kindred Spirits in the Grove

In the orchard, we conspire,
Planning tricks that never tire.
With apples in our hands we played,
The silly games that never fade.

We'd toss them high like flying dreams,
Laughter echoed, bursting seams.
A splat on someone's silly hat,
'Looks like you need a fruit combat!'

Ripe Reminders of Bygone Joys

Peaches rolling down the street,
The sound of laughter, oh so sweet!
With every bite, a giggle shared,
Memories made, no one was spared.

Nectarines slipped from our hold,
Each tumble brought a tale retold.
We laughed till we fell on the ground,
Where juicy treasures could be found.

A Bounty of Forgotten Smiles

Bananas stacked like jumbled dreams,
Each one whispered fruit-filled schemes.
We'd slip on peels, oh what a sight,
Rolling laughter, pure delight!

A fruit fight broke out in the sun,
Who knew such joy could be so fun?
And though we flung our bits away,
Those silly moments always stay.

Hidden Grove of the Heart

In a grove where laughter grows,
Jokes are ripened, sweet like prose.
Bananas peel back all the fun,
While apples giggle in the sun.

Grapes tell tales of green delight,
While cherries dance, oh what a sight!
Pineapple wears a crown so bright,
Spreading cheer both day and night.

Candor of Citrus

Lemons joke, with sour pouts,
Whisper secrets, share their doubts.
Oranges chuckle, zest is keen,
Making jokes, so fresh and clean.

Limes roll in, with a cheeky grin,
Puns on citrus, where to begin?
Grapefruit teases, oh what fun,
With every slice, the laughter's spun.

Still Life with Old Slices

Old slices lying in a heap,
Tell stories, make us laugh, not weep.
Moldy bread might bring some sighs,
But still, it wears a mask of lies.

Rotten apples, posing as kings,
Claiming titles, while laughter springs.
Tired pears with wrinkles galore,
Share laughs of youth, forevermore.

A Splash of Watermelon Wishes

Watermelon dreams come alive,
Juicy wishes in every slice.
Seeds of laughter scatter wide,
As summer's cheer we can't divide.

With each bite, a burst of glee,
A splash of juice, oh can't you see?
In this patch, where whimsy grows,
Laughter bubbles, and spontaneity flows.

Vines of Cherries and Dreams

In the garden of giggles grow,
Cherries ripe and laughter flow.
Each memory twirls like a vine,
A fruitcake dance, oh so divine.

Grandma's wig was a fruit parade,
With bananas and peaches displayed.
We thought her style was a big tease,
But she wore it with such great ease.

At the picnic, ants planned a raid,
On our snacks, a confection cascade.
We squealed as they marched with pride,
Thinking they'd steal the tart pie wide.

A tart fruit punch made us a mess,
Drenched in juice, we couldn't confess.
Laughter filled the sun-soaked day,
In cherry dreams, we danced away.

Sweet Surrender to Recollection

Once we peeled a grapefruit whole,
A sticky contest, oh what a goal!
Citrus juice dripped on our shoes,
Laughter erupted, we couldn't lose.

Mangoes tossed like footballs mailed,
While other kids just sadly failed.
We dodged the mess like champions right,
Our fruit-fueled games lasted till night.

Bananas split during the race,
One got stuck, a slippery face.
Racing to win, we slipped and squealed,
In the fruit saga, laughter was revealed.

Sweet memories, like berries, cling,
To the heart where joy does spring.
In every bite of the past, we find,
A fruity chuckle, two of a kind.

A Medley of Reminiscence

Peaches in a fruit fight flew,
Juices splashed, oh what a view!
Sticky fingers, laughter soared,
In memory's bowl, we were adored.

Watermelons carved into smiles,
Seed-spitting contests lasted for miles.
We'd giggle at the juice cascade,
As funny faces, not afraid were made.

In Grandma's kitchen, a blender roared,
Mixing fruits with laughs we stored.
We sipped our smoothies, tried to sing,
But ended up with fruity bling.

Old pies with quirky shapes, no doubt,
We dared to eat, though we should pout.
In a medley of mishaps and cheer,
The sweetest memories draw us near.

Citrus-Scented Echoes

Lemonade stood tall, a frothy crest,
But sour faces put it to the test.
One sip too bold, then a zesty fight,
As our laughter danced into the night.

Lime wedges became our little eyes,
Rolling forward in a soft disguise.
The dog gave chase as we burst with glee,
While citrus-stuck, we couldn't flee.

A grapefruit hat was a fashion hit,
For that one Sunny day, we were lit.
With giggles and smiles, we took our throne,
In citrus echoes, joy was sown.

Cherry bomb laughs in every slice,
Sweetened moments, oh, how nice.
In zest and jests, we bloom and grow,
Through the laughter, our spirits glow.

The Scent of Forgotten Seasons

In spring's embrace, the berries tease,
Plucking laughter from the trees.
Grapes whisper tales of summer's song,
While apples giggle, 'Come along!'

In autumn's coat, the pumpkins grin,
As Halloween brings a fruity spin.
Cider sings a merry tune,
While pears jump in their harvest moon.

Old cherries hide in jars so bright,
Their secrets burst with every bite.
Bananas blush with tales of shame,
As memories frolic, never tame.

When winter sneaks with frosty glee,
We chase our fruit from tree to tree.
A basket full of joy, you see,
In every bite, a comedy!

Citrus Hues of Reflection

A lemon twist, a zesty thought,
In citrus dreams, we all get caught.
Oranges laugh with every squeeze,
While tangerines do little tease.

The grapefruit flaunts its bitter wit,
While journeys swirl in every bit.
Limes roll in, uninvited surely,
Yet limey jokes come out purely.

In fruit stand banter, they unite,
With puns and zingers, what a sight!
A flavor clash, they throw a ball,
In fruity humor, we enthrall.

Each zest a spark, each squeeze a rhyme,
In fruity fun, we dance through time.
So let's make punch of all our fears,
And sip on laughs throughout the years!

Maraschino Memories

Oh maraschinos, bright and sweet,
With sugary tales, they can't be beat.
They sit atop a sundae high,
Winking cheekily at passersby.

Those cherries giggle with delight,
As whipped cream bounds, a fluffy sight.
A cherry pit, a game we play,
Whose spit can fly the farthest way?

In jello cups, they shake and jive,
While fuddled friends strive to survive.
With each dessert, a story grows,
As sweetness spills from nose to toes.

Every party's fruitcake make,
Holds memories sweet, none can mistake.
A maraschino romp, let's toast,
To fruity laughs—we love them most!

Carried by the Breeze

In orchards where the wind does play,
The fruits all dance in sunshine's ray.
Bananas swing from leafy vines,
While mangoes whisper silly lines.

The breeze brings tales from far away,
As peaches jest in summer's sway.
Pineapples wear their crowns with pride,
While coconuts just roll and hide.

A gentle gust, a playful shove,
As berries tumble, how we love!
Old fruit compacts spin like kites,
Bouncing high through sunny flights.

So take a seat, enjoy the show,
Where laughter blooms and breezes blow.
With every breath, the fruit parade,
Brings memories sweet that never fade!

Grapefruit Glow

In a world of citrus dreams,
Where grapefruits giggle and gleam,
I slipped on some juice, oh my fate!
Landed flat on a plate, what a scene!

With every slice, a laugh bestowed,
The tangy zest, my funny code,
I wore a fruit hat, quite a sight,
Under the sun, all fruity delight!

Friends gathered 'round, their faces bright,
With laughter peeling, it's pure delight,
We juggled oranges, a fumble parade,
One hit a tree, the whole thing swayed!

So here's to life with a spritz of cheer,
Squeezed memories soaked in good beer,
With grapefruit smiles that never fade,
Each silly moment, lovingly laid.

Memories Like Ripe Peaches

Peaches so plump, they dance at dawn,
Each bite a giggle, from dusk to yawn,
I once dropped one, it rolled away,
We chased it down, what a merry fray!

Sweet nectar drips, sticky as glue,
A marshmallow feast in a fruit stew,
Spinning round, on a pie we fell,
Laughter erupted, what a tale to tell!

Peach pits flying, quite a topping,
In a game of catch, eyebrows popping,
Every juicy jest, sunlight's embrace,
What a silly, heavenly place!

So let's toast to the fuzz and fun,
Where memories shine under the sun,
With peaches ripe and laughter grand,
A fruity fest, completely unplanned!

Cherry Blossom Afterglow

Oh how those cherries took to flight,
Dancing sweetly in the twilight,
A tree was pranked, its branches shook,
When a squirrel stole, oh what a crook!

Blossoms floated, like soft embrace,
Tickled my nose, what a funny chase,
Here comes a breeze, and oh what fun,
As I zigzagged, forget the run!

With cheeks full and silly delights,
We laughed till we cried, those starry nights,
The cherries giggled, perched on high,
As fireworks popped, brightening the sky!

So here's to the night, the bloom, the cheer,
Chasing laughter with friends all near,
In this garden where memories flow,
We'll dance and twirl in cherry glow!

Orchestra of the Orchard

In an orchard full of fruity tunes,
Apples are drumming beneath the moons,
Bananas are guitars, strumming away,
While pears sing loudly, come join the play!

The plums are dancers, twirling with glee,
As grapes are the crowd, just wait and see,
A watermelon solo, deep and profound,
Leaves a rhythm that's truly renowned!

Jokey oranges, with zestful flair,
Playing tricks, without a care,
The whole gang joins, in this fruity band,
Creating a memory, grand and unplanned!

So raise a glass, with fruit on the side,
As laughter and music blend and glide,
In this orchard where fun's the goal,
The sweetest symphony fills the soul!

Baskets Brimming with Inheritance

In the attic, jars of jam,
Grandma's prize, a fruity scam.
Each taste a giggle, a sweet delight,
Choking on laughter well into the night.

Peaches with tales, pears with pride,
Got my spoons, it's a wild ride.
A kiwi named Roger, never shuts up,
Sings in the corner, spilling the cup.

Uncle's red apples, dented and round,
Every bite holds a joke profound.
Cousins are bickering, seeds in the air,
Fruit fights erupt, not a single care.

Memories jigsawed in every slice,
Lemonade stand, oh, wasn't it nice?
Each treat is a giggle, a story anew,
In this basket of laughter, there's always room for two.

Whispers of Harvested Time

Bananas are talking, oh what a scene,
"They stole my shine!" says a grape so keen.
Soft laughter echoes from orange to pear,
Whispers of harvest float in the air.

Lemons chuckle while dancing around,
Throwing zest like confetti from the ground.
"Life's a fruit salad," they sing with glee,
If only they knew what follows me!

Pineapples boast of their prickly crown,
While berries complain they're the talk of the town.
A fruitarian comedy, full of cheer,
Their juicy secrets ringing in my ear.

Each pluck from the vine spins a new quirky tale,
Of wild fruit parties and grape-drunk ale.
In baskets of laughter, memories do rhyme,
Remnants of harvest, whispers of time.

Reflections in a Bowl of Fruit

In a bowl so bright, with colors so bold,
Fruits gather 'round, with stories to be told.
A cherry rolled in, with a giggling sound,
While an apple just whispered, "I'm homeward bound!"

The bananas are plotting to start a parade,
While plump berries wink, hoping for trade.
Each citrus speaks softly, secrets they share,
Reflections of laughter, floating in the air.

Grapes sing in harmony, each note a treat,
"Who needs a old song when you can tap your feet?"
Kiwis bounce lightly, spreading their cheer,
In the bowl of reflections, humor draws near.

From puns about fruit flies to tales of each tree,
These juicy encounters bring giggles to me.
Each slice of remembrance, a colorful spree,
In this bowl of hilarity, we're just meant to be.

Juxtaposed Memories of Flavor

In a tangle of flavors, unexpected and bright,
Strawberries quip, "We're leaders tonight!"
With jests made of sweetness, they flirt and they sway,
Juxtaposed flavors just brighten the day.

Lemons are sour, yet wise in their wit,
"I'm not just a garnish, I epitomize grit!"
Pineapples snicker at blueberries' fate,
Caught in a jam—oh, isn't that great?

A fruit salad quarrel, who's topping who's pie?
Cherries proclaim they could reach for the sky.
With crackers and cheese, a party unfolds,
As flavors collide like the tales we retold.

Each nibble a Joy, flavored with laughter,
Memories merge, oh, what comes after?
In a bowl of nonsense, flavors uplift,
Juxtaposed memories, our sweetest gift.

The Taste of Time

In the kitchen, a pie did gleam,
Filled with laughter, whipped cream.
My grandma danced with a fruity hat,
Juggling oranges, oh imagine that!

Time tickles like ripe cherries burst,
Each bite a memory, the sweet is worst.
We laughed till we cried, so absurdly right,
Mango mischief danced through the night.

Every taste brings back wild quests,
Like chasing plums, who knew that's the best?
Sticky fingers, running from bees,
Fruits of nostalgia, oh, how they tease!

Pineapple jokes served at the door,
Whispers of how we once wanted more.
Here's to our laughs and sweet delight,
Memories fruity, oh what a sight!

Sweet Nothings from the Past

Bananas peel, and giggles spill,
Candid tales that give a thrill.
The jammy days of our sticky youth,
Bringing forth those sweet, wild truths.

A watermelon seed, a launch to space,
Flew past my nose, oh what a race!
Grapes were battles, and lemons, jokes,
Handing out happiness, oh how it provokes!

From fruit fights to tart apple pie,
Every slice whispered a pie-in-the-sky.
We danced with peaches at the county fair,
In our berry-filled dreams, we floated in air.

Strawberries spoke in codes of delight,
Cherry bombs exploding in the night.
Life's a picnic with laughter in bulk,
Here's to the past — it's all fruit and silk!

Melon Moonlight

Under moonlit skies, we sliced up delight,
Melons laughing, oh such a sight!
Crimson juice ran down our chins,
Silly whispers, let the fun begin.

Cantaloupes rolling had us in stitches,
Tickling our toes, oh what rich niches!
We spun like the seeds, carefree and bright,
As shadows danced in the soft moonlight.

A melon ball party, quite out of hand,
Juggling our snacks, oh wasn't it grand?
Twirling and swirling, we crashed on the ground,
With giggles and memories, joy all around!

Each slice holds laughter that ripens with age,
Now, just a tale on a nostalgic page.
So here's to melons and those silly nights,
Bouncing through memories with laughter and light!

When Apples Were Gold

Once upon a time, apples gleamed bright,
They whispered secrets in the soft light.
We'd climb trees, brave and bold,
Shining visions — those treasures of gold!

Grapple with gravity, tumble, and roll,
Each crunchy bite filled up our soul.
Silly faces of cider-spilling bliss,
Who knew growing up would be like this?

Worms wore hats, played peek-a-boo games,
We laughed at mischief and silly names.
Every core told a story so wild,
Of youthful antics, free and wild.

So raise a toast with a crispy crunch,
To apple adventures, oh what a bunch!
When fruits were treasures we chased with glee,
Each bite a giggle, forever carefree!

Blossoms of Joy and Sorrow

In a garden of giggles, I found a pear,
Each bite came with laughter, floating in air.
A cherry burst forth with a sulky pout,
While lemons made jokes, just to hear us shout.

The berries would bicker, who's sweetest of all,
While grapes rolled in laughter, taking a fall.
A melon told stories, all juicy and bold,
As the plums whispered secrets, so sweet or so cold.

With every fresh slice, a new tale unfolds,
Tales of our childhood, in stories retold.
The pomegranate danced, in crimson flares,
While oranges and limes formed silly pairs.

As nostalgia ripened, with each silly scene,
We laughed 'til we cried, in this fruity routine.
So here in this garden, life's fun shall persist,
For the fruits of our memories, we can't resist.

Tart Tales from the Garden

Once a sour lemon tried to make a pie,
Claiming it was sweet, though we couldn't deny.
The raspberries giggled, while stuck in a jam,
And strawberries sneezed, saying, "Who gives a damn?"

In one corner, a fig wore a silly hat,
While cherries played cards with a playful cat.
Bananas did antics, slipping on the floor,
Causing a ruckus, then laughing for more.

A peach told a tale of a trip to the sea,
But it got sunburned, and now it's quite grumpy.
The apples all chuckled, with smiles so wide,
As they shared their own tales of fruit basket pride.

Amid all the fun in this comedic spree,
We learned fruit's not just snacks, but a family.
With puns traded sweetly, our laughter did start,
In the garden of memories, each day is an art.

The Apple of Remembrance

An apple sits proudly, in a shiny red guise,
It whispered one day, with mischievous eyes.
"I hold all the secrets of laughter and fun,
From picnics and parties, oh, and all that sun!"

It chuckled about days spent under the shade,
While making up stories, not one was dismayed.
With each juicy bite, more giggles would rise,
As the seeds of remembrance danced 'neath blue skies.

Now oranges piped in, with a zesty retort,
Claiming they held the best fruit-juicing sport.
But the kiwi just giggled, with fuzzy delight,
And told them, "You're all just a fruity insight!"

And thus in this orchard, tales flourish and bloom,
Where every fruit comes with a chuckle and room.
Together we savor, with banter as bliss,
For the apples of memory, we simply can't miss.

Melodies Under the Fig Tree

Under the fig tree, melodies play,
With fruits that are jamming, in their own fruity way.
The figs hold a concert, with notes in the air,
While bananas do the cha-cha, without a care.

A peach strums a banjo, so sweet and so round,
While oranges roll by, making laughable sounds.
The berries sing harmony, with giggles in tune,
And watermelon dances beneath the bright moon.

Together they laugh, and create quite a scene,
With each note of laughter, bursting so green.
In the shade of the leaves, where silliness reigns,
Their fruity ensemble binds all their chains.

So join in the laughter, every fruit has its place,
In this symphony sweet, we all find our space.
With melodies woven from joy and from glee,
In the heart of our garden, we're all fruity free.

Creamy Memories and Tangy Truths

In my fridge, there's a yogurt jar,
It's got a dance party, can't go far.
A spoonful of laughter, a dollop of cheer,
I might trip over it, but I have no fear.

Cherry jam whispers secrets in jars,
Dreaming of biscuits and candy bars.
The tang of the lemon, I just might miss,
While plotting my heist for a sweet, fruity kiss.

Pineapple slices wear crowns of gold,
Bragging rights rise as the stories unfold.
In this fruity circus, I'm the jester, you see,
I juggle my memories, sippin' iced tea.

Skipping through fruits, oh what a feat,
Mangoes are giggling, ain't life sweet?
With creamy delights and tangy zest,
I savor each moment, it's simply the best.

The Orchard's Silent Song

In an orchard of whispers, apples sneer,
They plot their escape with a wink and a cheer.
Peach trees sway, pretending to dance,
While nuts in the shells throw a wild prance.

Cherries giggle, as they dangle and swing,
On branches so tired, they hear freedom sing.
A ripe banana slips, with a cheeky grin,
It lands on the ground, letting laughter win.

The grapevines gossip in the warm sunny glow,
Making up stories only they know.
With a splash of surprise, they twirl and they whirl,
In this orchard of joy, let the memories unfurl.

Under the sun, the fruits play their part,
A symphony of flavors, a culinary art.
With silent songs, they share their sweet tales,
In a fruity paradise, where laughter prevails.

Whispers of Forgotten Flavors

Strawberries wear hats, it's a fanciful spree,
They gossip and giggle, just wait and see.
A raspberry blushes, so shy and coy,
In this secret garden, where fruits spread joy.

Pears tell tales of the days of yore,
When they danced on tables, wanting more.
But sticky caramel got stuck in a jam,
While the fruit-folk giggled at their bold slam.

Under the cabbage, a secret stash,
Of lemon meringue just waiting to clash.
With a wink and a nod, they make their stand,
This flavor fest is simply unplanned.

And in the chaos, old flavors rejoice,
Bouncing and bounding, they find their voice.
With whispers and giggles, old memories bloom,
In a fruity run riot, we shake off the gloom.

Tapestry of Sweet Reminiscence

Woven in laughter, a tapestry bright,
Fruits dance in circles, with glee and delight.
Lemons are sour, but don't make a fuss,
They add zest to life, giving us a plus.

Pineapples wear shades, looking oh-so-cool,
While melons on steps make a splash in the pool.
Berries trade jokes, so sweet and so sly,
As peaches chime in, "Oh, my, oh my!"

In this banquet of flavors, the laughter's the key,
Every bite's a chuckle, bursting with glee.
Fruit salads spin tales of joy and delight,
Each slice a memory, shining so bright.

So gather your laughter, your flavorful cheer,
Join the fruity fiesta, let go of your fear.
With a twist of the knife, and a wink of the eye,
This tapestry of moments will never say goodbye.

Lush Landscapes of Nostalgia

In the garden of laughter, time grows wide,
With wobbly trees that giggle and slide.
Each fruit bursts bright, a silly delight,
Like grandpa's old socks, a hilarious sight.

Berries wear hats, plums dance around,
While cherries throw pies, giggles abound.
Nostalgia's a prankster, with mischief in tow,
As we chase down memories, just like a show.

Bananas in pajamas, what a grand crew,
Each memory's quirkier than the last few.
With laughter as juice, I toast to the crew,
A feast of the past, all silliness true.

In this orchard of whimsy, we frolic and play,
Gathering fruits from yesterday's sway.
Each bite brings a chuckle, a twist of the past,
In the garden of giggles, we're meant to last.

Seeds of Longing

Planting wild thoughts in a patch of my mind,
With sprouting regrets, all tangled and blind.
Each seed's a memory, quirky and sweet,
Like the time that I tripped on my own silly feet.

Watered with laughter, they grow all around,
A kaleidoscope garden, with humor profound.
Papayas play poker, while grapefruit sings,
Mangoes in slippers do the silliest things.

Whimsical whispers rustle the trees,
Reminding me gently of childhood's unease.
A squirrel with a monocle, quite out of place,
Pretends he's the king at the fruit-flavored race.

So here's to the roots, their absurdity bright,
With memories twinkling, what a ridiculous sight!
As I cultivate dreams, a garden of cheer,
These seeds of my past will always be near.

The Color of Remembrance

Painting my thoughts with a brush of the past,
In hues of embarrassment, moments amassed.
Bright yellows of laughter, deep reds of despair,
  Mixed greens of mishaps, floating in air.

  Colorful echoes of giggles collide,
Like oranges and lemons that roll with the tide.
Memories dance wildly, a playful parade,
  Kiwis in tutus that never would fade.

Each stroke tells a story, a vibrant display,
With plump purple grapes, leading the way.
The canvas of yesterdays vivid and clear,
As I paint all my blunders, each joyful smear.

So let's savor the palette, of laughter and fun,
With flavors of friendship, a feast never done.
In a riot of colors, we giggle and cheer,
For the brightest of memories, forever held dear.

A Bowl of Sentiments

In a curious bowl, where feelings collide,
I find quirky fruits, with laughter as guide.
Pineapple grins, apples chuckle aloud,
While a cantaloupe wears a whimsical shroud.

Sentiments bubble like soda on ice,
Each fruit holds a story, oh isn't that nice?
With oranges that gossip and bananas that sing,
This mix of emotions is quite the wild fling.

A spoonful of whimsy ladles out dreams,
Wild memories bounce like a castle of seams.
Plums toss confetti, while striped kiwis prance,
In this playful bowl, join the silly dance!

So let's dig in deep, to savor the cheer,
With flavors of friendship, delicious and clear.
As we toss in our laughter and sprinkle our sighs,
This bowl of delights is a feast for the wise.

Memories in a Peeling Skin

I found a banana, ripe yet shifty,
Its laughter echoed, oh so nifty!
Peels flying high, a slippery play,
I slipped on giggles in a fruity ballet.

An orange chuckled, bursting with zest,
It told me stories, it did its best.
Lemonheads joined, with pucker so sweet,
We danced the tango, a citrus retreat.

A kiwi chimed in, fuzzy and bold,
Whispering secrets of ages untold.
With grapes in a bunch, we formed a parade,
In this joyful jam, no memories fade.

So here I stand, with peels all around,
Each laugh, each slip, leaves its mark profound.
In fruity fun, we twirl and we spin,
In this kicking chaos, let the party begin!

Candied Memories

A jar of sweets sits on the shelf,
Filled with laughter, who needs help?
Gummy bears giggle, oh what a sight,
Dancing like mad in sugar delight.

Chocolate bars whisper, rich and smooth,
Sharing their tales, trying to soothe.
Cotton candy clouds float on by,
Like sticky dreams in a candy sky.

Lollipops twirl with a playful grin,
Each flavor a memory, a win-win!
We swirl through the candy lands up high,
In sips of soda, fizzy and spry.

Let's wrap our past in syrup and cheer,
Making each moment perfectly clear.
With a crunch and a pop, we taste the bliss,
In this sugary world, nostalgia's a kiss!

Brewed in the Kitchen of Time

In a kettle bubbling, memories steep,
A pinch of laughter, a splash so deep.
Boiling over with stories untold,
Each sip of nostalgia is rich, manifold.

Tea bags of wisdom hang on the side,
While coffee beans unleash their pride.
Stirring in sugar, like a sweet delight,
We brew up the past, with flavor and light.

Cinnamon tales swirl in the steam,
Spices of humor mix in the dream.
From harried cooks to sizzling fun,
This kitchen of time never is done.

So ladle me laughter and pour out the joy,
A brew full of antics, oh what a ploy!
In every cup, let memories shine bright,
In this shared laughter, everything feels right.

Slices of Yesterday

Each slice of a sandwich hides tales to tell,
With peanut butter secrets, oh so swell.
Jelly giggles and crusty cheer,
Creating a feast when friends are near.

Tomatoes chuckle as they squish and pout,
Between bread and butter, they know what's up.
Lettuce leaps in with crunchy delight,
A salad of memories, fresh and bright.

Pickles pop in with a briny song,
Reminding us all where we belong.
With each bite a burst of flavors we find,
Our plates fill with laughter, it's one of a kind.

So let's raise a sandwich, toast to the past,
With flavors so rich, may the laughter last.
In every bite, let the memories play,
Celebrate the slices of yesterday!

Harvest of Reflections

In the fridge, fruit jostles about,
An apple says, "Let's go out!"
The bananas giggle, peel in a twist,
While cherries argue who's best on the list.

A grape rolls by, feeling so bold,
"I'm the best snack!" it loudly told.
But oranges just laugh, with zest so bright,
"You're just jelly! We're the real delight!"

Meanwhile, a pear with a dashing flair,
Practices dance moves, floating in the air.
The fruit mix all, in laughter and cheer,
As memories pile up, year after year.

So here's to our trips, both silly and sweet,
Where fruit and fun always compete.
With each quirky memory, we just can't quit,
To savor those moments, we'll always commit.

Echoes in the Orchard

In the orchard, apples flop down,
"Hey there, buddy!" they say with a frown.
Then suddenly, a pear falls with grace,
"Lemme just sit, I've run quite the race!"

Berries scatter, a raucous parade,
"Who's the juiciest?" in fruit-speak they trade.
A watermelon laughs, so big and round,
"Guess I'm the king, wear my crown proud!"

A banana slips by, on its top peel,
"I'm always on point, can I seal the deal?"
They giggle and bounce, with laughter so bright,
In this fruity world, everything feels right.

So gather your friends, let's join the fun,
Each fruit has a story; they weigh a ton.
Harvest the laughter, let it all blend,
These silly moments are what we commend.

Juicy Whispers of the Past

In the kitchen, fruits share a tale,
Mangoes shout, "I'm juicy, no fail!"
Kiwi whispers secrets, oh so absurd,
About the time a blender was stirred.

Pineapple chuckles, wearing a crown,
"Let's throw a party! No time for a frown!"
The strawberries blushed, feeling so bold,
"Our seeds are the best, if truth be told!"

A coconut nods, with a grin so wide,
"I've got the shell, the water inside!"
And as fruits bicker, in playful delight,
Their stories blend, like day into night.

So raise up your glasses, here's to the day,
When the fruits come alive, in their goofy way.
We'll cherish these moments, through laughter and cheer,

In the garden of memories, we hold dear.

Nostalgia in a Handful of Berries

Berries are bouncing, oh what a sight,
Blueberries brag, "We taste just right!"
Raspberries chime in, all sweet and fine,
"With our tartness, we truly outshine!"

Blackberries grumble, "Hey, give me a space!"
As strawberries dance all over the place.
A tussle erupts, who's the top pick?
In a swirl of laughter, it's all just a trick!

They reminisce of days spent under the sun,
Where juicy adventures were purely fun.
With each bite they take, memories flee,
Of summer days long gone, as sweet as can be.

So treasure these moments, in berry delight,
Let giggles and jests fill your heart up tight.
For every tiny fruit knows it plays a role,
In weaving our past with laughter and soul.

Citrus Sunshine on a Cloudy Day

A lemon peels with zest, you see,
It slips and slides so carelessly.
While oranges giggle, oh what a sight,
Dancing in the fridge, such pure delight.

The limes roll away, trying to hide,
In the shadows, where secrets abide.
Pineapple's crown, so proud and tall,
Tripping on grapes, they scatter and fall.

Mangoes chatter about the past,
Each tale funnier than the last.
Peachy faces blush with a grin,
As berry jokes begin to spin.

This fruity crew brings laughter near,
Juicy stories we all hold dear.
In the kitchen, the banter's insane,
Bringing sunshine, despite the rain.

Fragrances of Yesterday

A whiff of banana on a Tuesday night,
Calls forth laughter, oh what a fright!
Canned peaches whisper, soft and bright,
Sharing secrets in sweet moonlight.

Old apples reminisce with a sigh,
While cherries watch, their spirits high.
Apricots boast of their golden days,
In the fruit bowl, they sing and play.

The melon winks, it's so very sly,
Carving out jokes that make you cry.
As nuts laugh along, cracking right up,
In this garden of laughter, there's never a stop.

Memories swirl with a tangy taste,
As orange peels tumble in soft haste.
Time in the basket is a comedy show,
Each slice a giggle, the laughter will grow.

Time's Sweet Cravings

A fig waddles in, bringing snack time cheer,
Reminding us of that picnic last year.
With dates on a platter, oh what a treat,
Making us chuckle, oh so sweet!

The raspberry blushes, a shy little gem,
As Goji sings loudly, a musical hymn.
Kiwis and nuts play hopscotch at noon,
Bouncing and tumbling to a fruity tune.

Grapes spill tales of a vineyard race,
"I tripped on a vine and fell on my face!"
Bananas chuckle with their slippery tales,
While prunes share stories of past hiking trails.

Time may fly, but fruit keeps it light,
Jokes ripen sweetly, a pure delight.
With laughter and joy, cravings collide,
In this sweet realm, we take it all in stride.

Honeyed Echoes

Honey drips from memories bright,
Sweet on the tongue and airy in flight.
Nutty walnuts chuckle at every tease,
Dropping puns like leaves in the breeze.

Pears tell stories with juicy flair,
About wild adventures, none can compare.
The grapevine's gossip begins to sway,
Mighty fruit bonds in their funny play.

Melons wink with their cool, soft shroud,
Tickling the air, feeling quite proud.
Berries tease with a sprinkle of fun,
"Who's the sweetest? We all are, hon!"

With giggles and grins filling the space,
These honeyed echoes, we gladly embrace.
In every fruit, a laugh's hidden sweet,
Turning our hearts to the joys we repeat.

A Medley of Old Tastes

Once I had a peach so sweet,
It played a tune with each bite.
But every time I tried to eat,
A lemon zipped, what a sight!

Old banana, yellow and brown,
Tried to dance, slipped on the ground.
Grapes rolled by, with a little frown,
Making jelly, now that's profound!

Pineapples wore their spiky crowns,
Acting regal, oh what clowns!
Orange giggles in juicy gowns,
Made me laugh, I flipped and drowned!

In this bowl of kooky treats,
Each bite a joke, oh how it beats!
Memories of silly eats,
Echo in laughter, oh what feats!

Fragrant Sketches of the Past

A whiff of berries takes me there,
To childhood's joy, without a care.
Had a pie fight, what a flair,
Blueberries flew, can you declare?

Tart pineapple wore a grin,
With every slice, a playful spin.
Peaches chimed, let the fun begin,
I still find juice upon my chin!

Raspberries rolled, a daring race,
Made me trip, oh what disgrace!
But laughter healed the falling face,
I'd gladly join that messy chase!

Memories twirl in fruity jest,
Each flavor a laugh, we are blessed.
With every taste, I feel the zest,
In fragrant sketches, we invest!

Sunshine in a Jar

I once canned sunshine from a tree,
In jars it giggled just for me.
Pickled lemons, pure comedy,
They chuckled loud, what jolly spree!

A squeeze of lime and a wink of cheer,
Made pickle parties every year.
Tomatoes danced, full of good cheer,
In wooden spoons, they'd steer the sphere!

Mangoes sang in syrupy tones,
With every jar, they'd steal the bones.
But there's a fight 'tween stones and cones,
Running wild like noisy drones!

In jars of joy, memories gleam,
Each taste a quirky little dream.
Sunshine giggles, oh how they beam,
Delicious moments, glowing stream!

Cherries in the Wind

Cherries twirled, high in the breeze,
Playing tag with buzzing bees.
One took a dive, said, "Surprise!"
Landed in my fruit bowl's ease.

I tossed a grape, oh what a throw,
Olive winked, said, "Let it flow!"
Fig laughed so hard, rolled to and fro,
Singing songs of summers aglow!

Peaches plotted a grand escape,
Squeezing through with cheeky shape.
Nuts cracking jokes, oh the drape,
Of fruity fun that none can tape!

With every breeze, a fruit parade,
Laughter spills, in sunlight laid.
Cherries swirling, never fade,
In memories sweet, we've all stayed!

The Grappling of Time

In the orchard of moments, we frolic and slide,
Banana peels tossed, laughter our guide.
Time spins like a top, in a bright dizzy dance,
Chasing our shadows, in a silly romance.

Peaches whisper secrets, ripe with delight,
Each giggle we share, makes the wrongs feel right.
Bouncing through memories, like grapes on a vine,
Sipping on joy, like it's vintage fine wine.

Cherries in pockets, our treasures to keep,
Dancing through stories, in a watermelon leap.
With jelly bean wishes, we take to the sky,
In this grand comedy, we soar very high.

Time grapples and tumbles, with a mischievous grin,
As we juggle our memories, we dizzily spin.
No need for a stopwatch, just heartbeats will do,
In this ripe caper, it's all just for you.

Slices of Serenity

Peeling back layers, each slice tells a tale,
With mango musings, we set sail.
Papaya giggles float on the breeze,
As laughter and fruit blend with ease.

In the bowl of our being, strawberries shine,
Whipped cream cuddles, oh, how divine!
Plum puns abound, as we pop and we crack,
Joy served fresh, there's no need to hold back.

Kiwis do cartwheels, so bright and so bold,
Slicing through life, we share tales of old.
Pineapple crowns us, like jesters so grand,
In this circus of sweetness, we all make a stand.

With jests and with japes, the fruit tray we fling,
Sweet slices of laughter, we love everything.
In this fruity fiasco, we find our refrain,
Slicing through serenity, we dance in the rain.

Apricot Echoes

In the echo of apricots, laughter does bloom,
We juggle our memories, banishing gloom.
With zany tales of fruit fights and cheer,
Every juicy encounter brings us all near.

Puns ricochet off, like bouncy fruit balls,
Stories embedded within the walls.
Time softly shouts, with a chuckling tune,
We soar with our apricots, under the moon.

Silly faces made with a slice of peach,
Giggles that linger, just within reach.
From melon-head monsters to berry delight,
These echoes of joy keep our spirits alight.

So gather your friends for this fruity sweet song,
Where apricot echoes make us bounce along.
With every chuckle, in this whimsical spree,
We find that the fruit's just as funny as we!

Ripe Reflections in Twilight

As twilight descends, we gather 'round cheer,
With plump, juicy stories—the kind we hold dear.
A fig in each hand, and a grin on each face,
In ripe reflections, we relish our space.

Late nights filled with oranges, zestful and bright,
Sharing sweet tidbits, what a delightful sight!
Banter like berries, fresh off the vine,
In the twilight's embrace, our joy is divine.

Giggles and grapes, as our tales intertwine,
In this vintage of laughter, we simply recline.
A tapestry woven, of moments and fun,
Under the stars, our memories run.

So come raise a toast, with some fruit in your cup,
To ripe reflections, we're never grown-up!
In this merry gathering, with smiles so wide,
We savor each moment, with friends by our side.

An Apple's Whisper

An apple once said to a pear,
"Life's too juicy to worry and bear!"
With laughter they rolled in the sun,
Sipping sweet nectar, oh what fun!

A grape chimed in, plump and round,
"Let's dance on the table, it's safe and sound!"
While cherries giggled, one stole a kiss,
In the fruit bowl, who could resist?

Bananas slipped and created a fuss,
"Watch out, folks! I'm all over the bus!"
But laughter echoed, not a soul cared,
In the fruity kingdom, joy was shared.

So next time you munch on a snack,
Remember the fruit that had your back!
For in every bite, there's a tale to extract,
A giggle, a dance, and a funny pact.

When Fruit Brightened Days

On sunny mornings, berries would sing,
Reminding us all, life is a fling!
With strawberries chatting about a date,
And blueberries trading sweet cupcake fate.

The oranges rolled in, bright and bold,
"We're the sunshine, if I may be so told!"
In fruit bowl parlors, they'd toast with delight,
To the squishy mushiness of fruity bite!

Pineapple told tales of tropical woes,
"I got where I am with these prickly clothes!"
While mangoes danced with zest and flair,
"Join us in laughter, there's plenty to share!"

As lemons giggled, sour yet sweet,
Life was a party at every bite we meet!
So grab a fruit friend, join in the fun,
For in every memory, we've just begun.

Faded Recipes

Grandma had a cookbook, pages worn,
Filled with delights from the early morn!
But recipes faded with fruit of the years,
Now just a puzzle that brings on the tears.

"What's a dash of joy in a bowl full of zest?"
Asked the banana, curious and blessed!
A tangerine shrugged, "Was it a sprinkle of light?"
Or maybe a giggle, to make it taste right?

Lemons licked their lips at a jumbled list,
"I swear there was more in the twist of the mist!"
But in every mistake, there's a story we find,
Faded and jumbled, but oh so divine.

So let's spoon out the laughter, and slice any doubt,
For every old recipe brings giggles about!
In kitchens of whimsy, we bake with delight,
Creating new tales, every day, every night.

Almond Blossom Memories

In a garden of almonds, laughter would bloom,
As squirrels and birds filled the air with a tune!
"Do you recall our nutty escapades?"
Asked one to another, in sunny cascades.

"Remember the time we hid from the cat?"
Squeaked a small critter, looking quite fat!
"We climbed to the top; it was quite a thrill!"
As the cat made its move—what a dramatic spill!

Almond flowers danced in the warm summer breeze,
"Oh, the things we've done, let's reminisce, please!"
With each cheerful memory, the blossoms would sway,
Creating a symphony, come what may!

So when you bite into an almond surprise,
Remember the fun and the laughter that flies.
For in every crunch, a giggle takes flight,
In gardens of memories, shining so bright!

www.ingramcontent.com/pod-product-compliance
Lightning Source LLC
Chambersburg PA
CBHW051732290426
43661CB00122B/240